The Burning of Atlanta in 1864:
Cont

By Charles River Editors

A picture of civilians leaving Atlanta

About Charles River Editors

Charles River Editors was founded by Harvard and MIT alumni to provide superior editing and original writing services, with the expertise to create digital content for publishers across a vast range of subject matter. In addition to providing original digital content for third party publishers, Charles River Editors republishes civilization's greatest literary works, bringing them to a new generation via ebooks.

Sign up here to receive updates about free books as we publish them, and visit Our Kindle Author Page to browse today's free promotions and our most recently published Kindle titles.

Introduction

Sherman and his staff pose next to a cannon outside of Atlanta

The Burning of Atlanta

"We rode out of Atlanta by the Decatur road, filled by the marching troops and wagons of the Fourteenth Corps; and reaching the hill, just outside of the old rebel works, we naturally paused to look back upon the scenes of our past battles. We stood upon the very ground whereon was fought the bloody battle of July 22d, and could see the copse of wood where McPherson fell. Behind us lay Atlanta, smouldering and in ruins, the black smoke rising high in air, and hanging like a pall over the ruined city." - Sherman

After successfully breaking the Confederate siege at Chattanooga near the end of 1863, William Tecumseh Sherman united several Union armies in the Western theater for the Atlanta Campaign, forming one of the biggest armies in American history. After detaching troops for essential garrisons and minor operations, Sherman assembled his nearly 100,000 men and in May 1864 began his invasion of Georgia from Chattanooga, Tennessee, where his forces spanned a line roughly 500 miles wide.

. Sherman set his sights on the Confederacy's last major industrial city in the West and General Joseph E. Johnston's Army of Tennessee, which aimed to protect it. Atlanta's use to the Confederacy lay in its terminus for three major railroad lines that traveled across the South: the Georgia Railroad, Macon and Western, and the Western & Atlantic.[1] U.S. Lieutenant General Ulysses S. Grant knew this, sending Major General William Tecumseh Sherman's Division of the Mississippi towards Atlanta, with specific instructions, "get into the country as far as you can, inflicting all the damage you can against the war revenues."[2] The city's ability to send supplies to Lee's Army of Northern Virginia made Atlanta all the more important.

The timing of the invasion was also crucial. Throughout May 1864, Robert E. Lee skillfully stalemated Ulysses S. Grant in a series of battles known as the Overland Campaign, inflicting nearly 50,000 casualties on the Army of the Potomac. The casualties were so staggering that Grant was constantly derided as a butcher, and his lack of progress ensured that anti-war criticism of the Lincoln Administration continued into the summer before the presidential election. The Democrats nominated George McClellan, the former leader of the Army of the Potomac. McClellan had not been as aggressive as Lincoln hoped, but he was still exceedingly popular with Northern soldiers despite being fired twice, and the Democrats assumed that would make him a tough candidate against Lincoln. At the same time, Radical Republicans were still unsure of their support for Lincoln, and many begun running their own campaign against Lincoln for not prosecuting the war vigorously enough, urging Lincoln to withdraw from the campaign. The people of Atlanta clearly identified their own role in the struggle, as the *Atlanta Daily Appeal* noted, "The greatest battle of the war will probably be fought in the immediate vicinity of Atlanta. Its results determines that of the pending Northern Presidential election. If we are victorious the Peace party will triumph; Lincoln's Administration is a failure, and peace and Southern independence are the immediate results."[3]

It would fall upon Sherman's forces in the West to deliver the necessary victory. Johnston's army of 50,000 found itself confronted by almost double its numbers, and General Johnston began gradually retreating in the face of Sherman's forces, despite repulsing them in initial skirmishes at Resaca and Dalton. The cautious Johnston was eventually sacked and replaced by the more aggressive John Bell Hood once the Confederate army was back in Atlanta. Taking command in early July 1864, Hood lashed out at Sherman's armies with several frontal assaults on various portions of Sherman's line, but the assaults were repulsed, particularly at Peachtree

---

[1] National Park Service, "Genesis in Steel: Railroads Build a City," in *Campaign for Atlanta*, http://www.nps.gov/history/history/online_books/civil_war_series/7/sec1.htm#1

[2] Ecelbarger, *The Day Dixie Died*, 9.

[3] Ecelbarger, *The Day Dixie Died*, 11.

Creek on July 20, where George H. Thomas' defenses hammered Hood's attack. At the same time, Sherman was unable to gain any tactical advantages when attacking north and east of Atlanta.

In August, Sherman moved his forces west across Atlanta and then south of it, positioning his men to cut off Atlanta's supply lines and railroads. When the Confederate attempts to stop the maneuvering failed, the writing was on the wall. On September 1, 1864, Hood and the Army of Tennessee evacuated Atlanta and torched everything of military value. On September 3, 1864, Sherman famously telegrammed Lincoln, "Atlanta is ours and fairly won." Two months later, so was Lincoln's reelection.

Sherman has earned fame and infamy for being the one to bring total war to the South, and it started at Atlanta. Once his men entered the city, Sherman ordered the 1,600 citizens remaining in Atlanta to evacuate the city as he, in Grant's words, set out to "destroy [Atlanta] so far as to render it worthless for military purposes," with Sherman himself remaining a day longer to supervise the destruction himself "and see that it was well done."[4] Then on November 14, 1864, Sherman abandoned the ravaged city, taking with him thirteen thousand mules and horses and all the supplies the animals could carry.

One of the most famous movies of all time, *Gone With The Wind*, depicts the burning of Atlanta after Sherman occupied it in 1864. Over time, history came to view Sherman as a harbinger of total war, and in the South, Sherman is still viewed as a brutal warmonger. Considerable parts of Atlanta and Columbia did burn when Sherman occupied them in 1864 and 1865 respectively, but how responsible was Sherman for the initial fires?

To this day, there is no definitive answer. As part of its retreat out of Atlanta, Confederate forces were ordered to burn anything of military value to keep it from falling into the hands of Sherman's army. Inevitably, those fires did not stay contained, damaging more than their intended targets. In November, preparing for the March to the Sea, Sherman similarly ordered everything of military value burned. Those fires also spread, eventually burning much of Atlanta to the ground. When Sherman's men left, only 400 buildings were left standing in the city.

Due in large part to his actions in Georgia, Sherman remains controversial across much of the United States today. He was unquestionably instrumental at battles like Shiloh, his victory in the Atlanta Campaign reassured Lincoln's reelection, and his March to the Sea revolutionized total warfare. At the same time, the South considered him akin to a terrorist and adamantly insisted that he was violating the norms of warfare by targeting civilians. In many ways, Sherman is still the scourge of the South over 150 years after he vowed to make Georgia howl.

---

4   Grant, U. S. (John. Y. Simon, editor). *Ulysses S. Grant: Memoirs and Selected Letters.* Page 642.

A picture of "Sherman's neckties," a colloquial term for destroyed railroad lines

The Burning of Atlanta in 1864: The History of One of the Civil War's Most Controversial Events

About Charles River Editors

Introduction

Chapter 1: Preparing for the Campaign

Chapter 2: Taking Atlanta

Chapter 3: The Union Occupation of Atlanta

Chapter 4: Leaving Atlanta in Ruins

Online Resources

Bibliography

Chapter 1: Preparing for the Campaign

Atlanta's railyards in 1864.

Sherman's Atlanta Campaign was one of the most famous and decisive campaigns of the entire Civil War, but the success was only made possible after he and Ulysses S. Grant had overseen the lifting of the Confederate siege of Chattanooga after the Battle of Chickamauga. As a result, Sherman would start his Atlanta Campaign using Chattanooga as his main supply and communications base, and he would launch that campaign with more than twice as many men at his disposal than the Army of Tennessee, which would start the campaign commanded by Joseph Johnston. Johnston, the man Longstreet had suggested to replace Bragg, would eventually be named commander after Bragg offered his resignation of the command near the end of 1863 and his friend Jefferson Davis accepted it (to Bragg's surprise).

Grant

During the Civil War, one of the tales that was often told among Confederate soldiers was that Joseph E. Johnston was a crack shot who was a better bird hunter than just about everyone else in the South. However, as the story went, Johnston would never take the shot when asked to, complaining that something was wrong with the situation that prevented him from being able to shoot the bird when it was time. The story is almost certainly apocryphal, but it was aptly used to demonstrate the Confederates' frustration with a man who everyone regarded as a capable general. Johnston began the Civil War as one of the South's senior commanders, leading the ironically named Army of the Potomac to victory in the Battle of First Bull Run over Irvin McDowell's Union Army. But Johnston would become known more for losing by not winning.

Johnston was never badly beaten in battle, but he had a habit of strategically withdrawing until he had nowhere left to retreat. When Johnston had retreated in the face of McClellan's army before Richmond in 1862, he finally launched a complex attack that not only failed but left him severely wounded, forcing him to turn over command of the Army of Northern Virginia to Robert E. Lee. Johnston and Confederate President Jefferson Davis had a volatile relationship throughout the war, but Johnston was too valuable to leave out of service, so he found himself in command of the Army of Tennessee at the beginning of 1864.

Johnston

Failing to secure the capture of any major Northern cities, or the recognition of Great Britain or France, or the complete destruction of any Northern armies, the Confederacy's last chance to survive the Civil War was the election of 1864. Democrats had been pushing an anti-war stance or at least a stance calling for a negotiated peace for years, so the South hoped that if a Democrat defeated President Lincoln, or if anti-war Democrats could retake the Congress, the North might negotiate peace with the South. In the election of 1862, anti-war Democrats made some gains in Congress and won the governorship of the State of New York, so Confederates were hopeful that trend would continue in the election of 1864.

Before beginning the Overland Campaign against Lee's army, Grant, Sherman and Lincoln devised a new strategy that would eventually implement total war tactics. Grant aimed to use the Army of the Potomac to attack Lee and/or take Richmond. Meanwhile, General Sherman, now in command of the Department of the West, would attempt to take Atlanta and strike through Georgia. In essence, having already cut the Confederacy in half with Vicksburg campaign, he now intended to bisect the eastern half.

On top of all that, Grant and Sherman were now intent on fully depriving the Confederacy of the ability to keep fighting. Sherman put this policy in effect during his March to the Sea by confiscating civilian resources and literally taking the fight to the Southern people. For Grant, it meant a war of attrition that would steadily bleed Lee's Army of Northern Virginia. To take full advantage of the North's manpower, the Union ended prisoner exchanges in 1864 in an attempt to ensure that the Confederate armies could not be bolstered by paroled prisoners.

Sherman

Major General Sherman's Division of the Mississippi had within its organization three armies, all taking their names from rivers West: the Army of the Tennessee, the Army of the Cumberland, and the Army of the Ohio. Each command and corps consisted of veterans who fought in Union victories at Shiloh, Corinth, Vicksburg, and Chattanooga, so they were confident at the start of the summer that they would ultimately reach Atlanta. Their commander was also confident, as Sherman later recalled in his memoirs, "The next spring when I was in Chattanooga, preparing for the Atlanta campaign, Corporal Pike made his appearance and asked a fulfillment of my promise. I inquired what he wanted, and he said he wanted to do something bold, something that would make him a hero. I explained to him, that we were getting ready to go for Joe Johnston at Dalton, that I expected to be in the neighborhood of Atlanta about the 4th of July..."

In April 1864, Grant gave fairly discretionary orders to Sherman: "You I propose to move against Johnston's army, to break it up, and to get into the interior of the enemy's country as far as you can, inflicting all the damage you can against their war resources. I do not propose to lay down for you a plan of campaign, but simply to lay down the work it is desirable to have done, and leave you free to execute it in your own way. Submit to me, however, as early as you can, your plan of operations." Sherman replied with a general outline of his proposed movements and what he expected Johnston would do:

> "It will take us all of April to get in our furloughed veterans, to bring up A. J. Smith's command, and to collect provisions and cattle on the line of the Tennessee. Each of the armies will guard, by detachments of its own, its rear communications.

> At the signal to be given by you, Schofield, leaving a select garrison at Knoxville and London, with twelve thousand men will drop down to the Hiawassee, and march against Johnston's right by the old Federal road. Stoneman, now in Kentucky, organizing the cavalry forces of the Army of the Ohio, will operate with Schofield on his left front—it may be, pushing a select body of about two thousand cavalry by Ducktown or Elijah toward Athens, Georgia.

> Thomas will aim to have forty-five thousand men of all arms, and move straight against Johnston, wherever he may be, fighting him cautiously, persistently, and to the best advantage. He will have two divisions of cavalry, to take advantage of any offering.

> McPherson will have nine divisions of the Army of the Tennessee, if A. J. Smith gets here, in which case he will have full thirty thousand of the best men in America. He will cross the Tennessee at Decatur and Whitesburg, march toward Rome, and feel for Thomas. If Johnston falls behind the Coosa, then McPherson will push for Rome; and if Johnston falls behind the Chattahoochee, as I believe he will, then McPherson will cross over and join Thomas...

> Should Johnston fall behind the Chattahoochee, I will feign to the right, but pass to the left and act against Atlanta or its eastern communications, according to developed facts.

> This is about as far ahead as I feel disposed, to look, but I will ever bear in mind that Johnston is at all times to be kept so busy that he cannot in any event send any part of his command against you or Banks."

Thomas

Sherman also informed Grant that he fully intended to provision his own army by living off the land, a crucial component of their total war strategy: "If Banks can at the same time carry Mobile and open up the Alabama River, he will in a measure solve the most difficult part of my problem, viz., 'provisions.' But in that I must venture. Georgia has a million of inhabitants. If they can live, we should not starve. If the enemy interrupt our communications, I will be absolved from all obligations to subsist on our own resources, and will feel perfectly justified in taking whatever and wherever we can find. I will inspire my command, if successful, with the feeling that beef and salt are all that is absolutely necessary to life, and that parched corn once fed General Jackson's army on that very ground."

Chapter 2: Taking Atlanta

As Johnston continued to gradually move south, and thus closer to Atlanta, people were growing increasingly worried. "In Richmond, Jefferson Davis began to grow uneasy. So did many other Southerners, particularly those in Georgia, and above all those in Atlanta. When and where would Johnston stand and fight Sherman? Would he stand and fight him at all?"[5] At the same time, however, Johnston's choice of retreat also concerned Sherman, and previous fighting had convinced the Union commander that he should take advantage of the large size of his armies and outflank Johnston, with the intention of marching on Dallas, Georgia.

Johnston may have left his superiors and subordinates upset, but he continued to successfully keep his army between Sherman and Atlanta, and the terrain of Georgia still offered him the best defense. Brushy, Pine, and Lost Mountains all served as fortified areas to prevent Sherman any quick way to Atlanta, and on June 9, Union advance ground to a halt. It would have despaired Johnston to learn that logistical issues and an increase in manpower were the reasons for the halt; since Sherman wanted to advance along the Western & Atlantic railroad, the Union forces needed to complete a railroad over the Etowah River. That pause gave time to add the XVII Corps of the Army of the Tennessee to the picture. In four days, the arrival of these two divisions, commanded by Major General Francis P. Blair, Jr, replaced the Union losses of the last month.

By July, General-in-Chief Henry Halleck notified Sherman at this time that the imminent battle for Atlanta now assumed priority status in the greater overall Union strategy to win the war. Grant had failed to achieve a knockout blow against Lee, and the Army of the Potomac no longer possessed an offensive capability thanks to losses of 60,000 soldiers, killed or wounded during the Overland Campaign. This meant Grant could ill-afford to chance a pivotal defeat, especially as the election was approaching, one that had taken on the appearance of a referendum on the continuation of the war itself. Copperheads, pro-Southern Democrats who advocated Confederate separatism, a larger population of aggrieved families weary of more bloodshed, and a worthy challenger to Lincoln's presidency in the form of Major General George B. McClellan, all seemed to suggest Lincoln could lose. At the very least, these factors gave the appearance that if Union armies suffered one more costly and inconclusive engagement with the rebels, the people of the Union would overwhelmingly choose a plan of peace, if not reconciliation, with the South and defeat Lincoln at the polls. For these reasons, Sherman and his men truly believed that they had to capture Atlanta or decisively defeat the Army of Tennessee in a conclusive battle before the elections in November if the Union was to win the war.

Meanwhile, events beyond Sherman's control shaped how the great drama for control of Atlanta would play out. Although Johnston's tactics were by all accounts "brilliantly planned and

---

[5] "The Campaign for Atlanta (From the Oostanaula to the Etowah)," National Park Service: The Civil War Series (History E-Library), http://www.nps.gov/history/history/online_books/civil_war_series/7/sec3.htm

executed," Sherman's refusal to give battle foiled the strategy Johnston hoped to use, and it completely unnerved President Jefferson Davis. It also upset some of his own subordinates, most notably John Bell Hood. Ironically, the one attempt Johnston made to take an offensive tact during the Battle of Adairsville had been foiled by Hood himself, but regardless, many Confederates feared Johnston was squandering the great opportunity provided by the defense of Richmond. If Johnston continued his pattern of withdrawals and lost Atlanta, then the plan of the Confederacy to win the war by not losing would be wasted.

Hood

Fearing Johnston would give up Atlanta without a fight, Davis telegraphed Johnston to ask what he planned to do to stop Sherman. Already cultivating a decidedly hostile attitude toward the misguided Davis, a thought came to mind that spurred further distrust from Johnston. Earlier in the war, when General "Fightin' Joe" Wheeler had confided his battle strategy to Davis, it appeared verbatim in the Richmond newspapers the next day. Thus, Johnston was intentionally evasive, responding that he would fight Sherman whenever he saw a chance to do so with advantage.

Ultimately, Davis sent his chief-of-staff, General Braxton Bragg, to Atlanta, to ascertain Johnston's plans. Perhaps Davis knew what he would find due to his previous dealings with Johnston during the Peninsula Campaign in 1862, when Johnston needed prodding to come out from behind his defenses and fight the Army of the Potomac. The two were also at odds over the ill-fated defense of the Mississippi city of Vicksburg, when Johnston failed to relieve the siege of the last Confederate stronghold on the Mississippi River. On top of all of Davis's dealings with a general who gave more excuses than battles, Johnston never communicated well with Davis; urgings for reports from the recalcitrant general usually resulted in one paragraph responses – if any response at all.

Davis and Johnson clearly had a rocky relationship, and as the Army of Tennessee continued withdrawing until it had crossed the last major water barrier before Atlanta (the Chattahoochee River), General Hood was covertly sending letters to the command center at Richmond that were very critical of Johnston's conduct. After meeting with Johnston, Bragg then sat with Hood and another subordinate, Joseph Wheeler, who both reported they had repeatedly urged Johnston to go on the attack rather than allow Sherman to dominate the battlefield. Hood presented a damning letter that characterized Johnston as "ineffective and weak-willed," telling Bragg, "I have, General, so often urged that we should force the enemy to give us battle as to almost be regarded reckless by the officers high in rank in this army, since their views have been so directly opposite."

Perhaps not surprisingly, Davis did not like what he heard from Atlanta. Bragg's report described a panicked city, and he noted that Johnston gave little away about his plans. All Bragg saw was, in his opinion, a commanding general willing to give up the city. Making matters worse for himself, Johnston wanted Nathan Bedford Forrest's cavalry, busy in the defense of eastern Mississippi and northern Alabama, to come to his aid in Atlanta, in effect, giving up Forest's hard-fought territory that was vital to the supply of the Army of Tennessee. That request from Johnston may have made up Davis's mind, but Davis personally wrote to Johnston for the divulgement of plans. Johnston responded, "As the enemy has double our number, we must be on the defense. My plan of operations must, therefore, depend on that of the enemy. It is mainly to watch for an opportunity to fight to advantage. We are trying to put Atlanta in condition to be held for a day or two by the Georgia militia, that army movements may be freer and wider."[6]

Davis did not want to hear that Johnston would use militia to defend Atlanta while Johnston left the city to supposedly go on the offensive against an enemy that Johnston had already proved reluctant to attack, not to mention one that Johnston noted was so much bigger than his own. When Johnston wrote another letter telling Davis that preparations should be made for the abandonment of Andersonville, the notorious prisoner-of-war camp in southern Georgia more than one hundred miles south of Atlanta, Davis had heard enough. On the morning of July 17, Davis made his decision, and that afternoon, two telegrams arrived in Atlanta: one for Johnston, one for Hood.

---

[6] "Across the Chattahoochee (July 3-17)," *Civil War Series (The Campaign for Atlanta),* National Park Service., http://www.nps.gov/history/history/online_books/civil_war_series/7/sec6.htm

The telegram Johnston received read, "Lieutenant-General J. B. Hood has been commissioned to the temporary rank of general, under the late law of Congress. I am directed by the Secretary of War to inform you that, as you have failed to arrest the advance of the enemy to the vicinity of Atlanta, far in the interior of Georgia, and express no confidence that you can defeat or repel him, you are hereby relieved from the command of the Army and Department of Tennessee, which you will immediately turn over to General Hood." [7]

Johnston immediately fired back with a retort pointing out that in actuality, General Sherman had come no closer to Atlanta than Grant had come to Richmond, adding, "Your dispatch of yesterday received and obeyed. Command of the Army and Department of Tennessee has been transferred to General Hood. As to the alleged cause of my removal, I assert that Sherman's army is much stronger compared with that of Tennessee, than Grant's compared with that of Northern Virginia. Yet the enemy has been compelled to advance much more slowly to the vicinity of Atlanta, than to that of Richmond and Petersburg; and penetrated much deeper into Virginia than into Georgia. Confident language by a military commander is not usually regarded as evidence of competence."[8]

Johnston would later sum up his view of the Atlanta Campaign while he was in command: "No material was lost by us in the campaign, but the four field-pieces exposed and abandoned at Resaca by General Hood. The troops themselves, who had been seventy-four days in the immediate presence of the enemy; laboring and fighting daily; enduring toil and encountering danger with equal cheerfulness; more confident and high-spirited even than when the Federal army presented itself before them at Dalton; and, though I say it, full of devotion to him who had commanded them, and belief of ultimate success in the campaign, were then inferior to none who ever served the Confederacy, or fought on this continent."

At just 33 years old, Hood was now the youngest man on either side of the conflict to be given full command of an army. Robert E. Lee gave an enthusiastic reply to Hood's promotion, calling Hood "a bold fighter, very industrious on the battlefield, careless off."[9] Hood had fought valiantly at Antietam, Gettysburg, and Chickamauga, suffering a debilitating arm injury and losing a leg. Hood was a popular figure in the South, where he was widely viewed as both gallant and chivalrous (Mary Chesnut wrote in her famous diary that Hood was "a beau-ideal of the wild Texans"), but he was also one of the most tenacious generals in the Confederacy, for better and worse. This quality, which made him one of the best brigade and division commanders in the Army of Northern Virginia, also rendered him ineffective when he was promoted to higher commands like the one he had just received. With his crippled arm tucked in his shirt and an

[7] Johnston, Joseph, *Narrative of Military Operations; Directed, During the Late War Between the States*, 349, https://archive.org/stream/narrativeofmilit00john/narrativeofmilit00john_djvu.txt

[8] Johnston, Joseph, *Narrative of Military Operations; Directed, During the Late War Between the States*, 349, https://archive.org/stream/narrativeofmilit00john/narrativeofmilit00john_djvu.txt

[9] Woodworth, Steven E. *Jefferson Davis and His Generals: The Failure of Confederate Command in the West.* Pages 284—285.

empty trouser leg pinned to his thigh, General Hood would conduct the remainder of the Atlanta Campaign with the strong and aggressive actions for which he had become famous.

From the beginning, Hood sensed an opportunity for offensive operations because Sherman had divided up his armies, and Hood perceived a gap existed between Schofield and McPherson (who both moved east of Atlanta) and Thomas, who now moved across Peachtree Creek. The gap existed due to Sherman's decision to cut the rail line to the east, which would create a longer period of time for any possible reinforcements to arrive from Richmond, and vice versa. He also meant to move his army into the lands that supplied Atlanta; if Sherman could cut off eastern Georgia, an agricultural belt that stretched from Atlanta to Savannah, the army and citizens inside Atlanta could be starved out.

McPherson

In the end, the Army of Tennessee simply lacked the offensive power to defeat the combined strength of Sherman's numbers. The Battle of Peachtree Creek inflicted nearly 2,500 Confederate casualties and 2,000 Northern casualties.[10]

Hood and the Army of Tennessee had not defeated the invading Union armies, but their aggressive moves did mean that Sherman still failed to break the last railroad, the Macon, between Atlanta and the South. In Richmond, the Southern press was selective in the news they printed, giving the appearance upon first reading that the Confederacy still survived in Georgia and its fighting forces could still achieve a future victory that would force Lincoln and his government to lose the election and preserve the independence of the Southern Confederacy. However, news of the horrific losses at Peachtree Creek sickened the people of the South.

Back in Atlanta, Hood still had to figure out how to stop Sherman's armies. Due to earlier attempts to approach the city in the north and east, Hood wisely guessed the direction from which Sherman would move in an effort to break the railroad. With the intention of breaking the Union armies once and for all, Hood came up with another aggressive and complicated plan that, one claimed, looked as if Hood was dreaming up the late, great General Stonewall Jackson. When and if Sherman transferred the army that could make the movement, the Army of the Tennessee, two corps, led by Lieutenant General Stephen D. Lee and Lieutenant General Alexander P. Stewart, would simultaneously hold the Army of the Tennessee while performing a great sweeping movement to fall upon the army's rear and destroy it.

On August 30, Hood believed he understood Sherman's plans upon hearing from what remained from his cavalry that the Army of the Tennessee had approached Jonesboro. To crush Sherman, Hood ordered Hardee and Lee's corps to attack, with explicit orders to drive the federals across the Flint River. Hood's plan was incredibly ambitious, as it relied on Lee needing to lead his half-starved forces on a three day march that to join in the battle with Hardee's corps. By the time the Confederates were ready to attack Howard and his men, the Union army was well-fortified and ready for any assault. Logan's XV Corps faced most of the fight, and the sides were evenly matched with about 20,000 soldiers each, but the footsore and demoralized rebels were repeatedly repulsed. Lee's corps faced the worst of the losses, with 1400 casualties out of the 2200 who had fought.

When Hood heard the report of Hardee and Lee's defeat, which he had to receive from a courier because Sherman had cut the telegraph along with the last railroad, he finally realized he could not defend Atlanta. Worried that he would lose the entire Army of Tennessee if the Union armies tightened the grip on the city, he ordered the retreat to begin on September 1. Hood would later complain in his memoirs that Sherman justified the subsequent destruction of Atlanta based on a false depiction of Atlanta as being militarily formidable: "Atlanta could not properly be designated a regularly fortified city. It was simply protected by temporary breastworks, of the same character as those used by Johnston and Sherman, during the preceding campaign. The fortifications consisted of a ditch, with a log to act as protection to the heads of the men whilst firing, and of brushwood, when it could be obtained, thrown out in front as an obstruction to a

[10] "Battle of Peachtree Creek," About Northern Georgia,
http://www.aboutnorthgeorgia.com/ang/Battle_of_Peachtree_Creek

rapid advance of the enemy. A large portion of the line, which passed through open fields, was devoid of this latter safeguard. Moreover, only a few of the heavy guns and batteries were covered by embankments with embrasures. It might be supposed, from General Sherman's Memoirs, that Atlanta was not only a thoroughly fortified town, but was provisioned to endure a siege of a year or more, after all communication was cut off; that it possessed arsenals and machine shops as extensive as those in Richmond and Macon — an illusion created, probably, by a dilapidated foundry, near the Augusta road, which had been in use prior to the war. General Sherman, therefore, cannot assert, in order to justify certain acts, that Atlanta was a regularly fortified town. And whereas I marched out at night, allowing him the following day to enter the city, unopposed, as he himself acknowledges, and whereas no provocation was given by the authorities, civil or military, he can in no manner claim that extreme war measures were a necessity."

A picture of tracks ruined by the retreating Confederates

For his part, Sherman noted that the first truly intentional acts of destruction in Atlanta were carried out by Confederates the night they retreated: "About 2 o'clock that night the sounds of heavy explosions were heard in the direction of Atlanta, distant about twenty miles, with a succession of minor explosions and what seemed like the rapid firing of cannon and musketry. These continued about an hour, and again about 4 a.m. occurred another series of similar discharges apparently nearer us, and these sounds could be accounted for on no other hypothesis than of a night attack on Atlanta by General Slocum or the blowing up of the enemy s magazines."

Sherman would attempt to give chase later, but two things prevented him from the objective of destroying the Army of Tennessee. The defenses that Hardee had put in place around Lovejoy's Station were too strong to risk an attack, but more importantly, Sherman's soldiers were on the cusp of fulfilling a goal that would cause celebrations in the North. Major General Henry B. Slocum and his XX Corps had cautiously moved forward into Atlanta's defenses until noticing that the Confederate army had abandoned the city, which compelled Sherman to send one of the most famous messages of the war to the War Department in Washington, D.C.:[11]

"[R]umors came from the rear that the enemy had evacuated Atlanta, and that General Slocum was in the city. Later in the day I received a note in Slocum's own handwriting, stating that he had heard during the night the very sounds that I have referred to; that he had moved rapidly up from the bridge about daylight, and had entered Atlanta unopposed. His letter was dated inside the city, so there was no doubt of the fact. General Thomas's bivouac was but a short distance from mine, and, before giving notice to the army in general orders, I sent one of my staff-officers to show him the note. In a few minutes the officer returned, soon followed by Thomas himself, who again examined the note, so as to be perfectly certain that it was genuine. The news seemed to him too good to be true. He snapped his fingers, whistled, and almost danced, and, as the news spread to the army, the shouts that arose from our men, the wild hallooing and glorious laughter, were to us a full recompense for the labor and toils and hardships through which we had passed in the previous three months."

"A courier-line was at once organized, messages were sent back and forth from our camp at Lovejoy's to Atlanta, and to our telegraph-station at the Chattahoochee bridge. Of course, the glad tidings flew on the wings of electricity to all parts of the North, where the people had patiently awaited news of their husbands, sons, and brothers, away down in 'Dixie Land;' and congratulations came pouring back full of good-will and patriotism. This victory was most opportune; Mr. Lincoln himself told me afterward that even he had previously felt in doubt, for the summer was fast passing away; that General Grant seemed to be checkmated about Richmond and Petersburg, and my army seemed to have run up against an impassable barrier, when, suddenly and unexpectedly, came the news

[11] "Atlanta is Ours," *Civil War Series (The Campaign for Atlanta)*, National Park Service, http://www.nps.gov/history/history/online_books/civil_war_series/7/sec13.htm;

that 'Atlanta was ours, and fairly won.' On this text many a fine speech was made, but none more eloquent than that by Edward Everett, in Boston. A presidential election then agitated the North. Mr. Lincoln represented the national cause, and General McClellan had accepted the nomination of the Democratic party, whose platform was that the war was a failure, and that it was better to allow the South to go free to establish a separate government, whose corner-stone should be slavery. Success to our arms at that instant was therefore a political necessity; and it was all-important that something startling in our interest should occur before the election in November. The brilliant success at Atlanta filled that requirement, and made the election of Mr. Lincoln certain. Among the many letters of congratulation received, those of Mr. Lincoln and General Grant seem most important:

EXECUTIVE MANSION

WASHINGTON, D.C. September 3, 1864.

The national thanks are rendered by the President to Major-General W. T. Sherman and the gallant officers and soldiers of his command before Atlanta, for the distinguished ability and perseverance displayed in the campaign in Georgia, which, under Divine favor, has resulted in the capture of Atlanta. The marches, battles, sieges, and other military operations, that have signalized the campaign, must render it famous in the annals of war, and have entitled those who have participated therein to the applause and thanks of the nation.

ABRAHAM LINCOLN

President of the United States

CITY POINT VIRGINIA, September 4, 1864-9 P.M.

Major-General SHERMAN: I have just received your dispatch announcing the capture of Atlanta. In honor of your great victory, I have ordered a salute to be fired with shotted guns from every battery bearing upon the enemy. The salute will be fired within an hour, amid great rejoicing.

U. S. GRANT, Lieutenant-General."[12]

A picture of Union soldiers destroying tracks outside Atlanta

---

[12] *Memoirs of General Sherman,* http://www.gutenberg.org/files/4361/4361-h/4361-h.htm

A picture of a Union camp by Atlanta's City Hall

"No officer should allow his soldiers to bum and pillage after victory has been secured." – John Bell Hood

The campaign had ended, but the fighting did not, and things were only about to get worse for Atlanta. To begin with, Sherman planned to expel the citizens of Atlanta; he did not want to feed them, nor did he entirely trust them, and either way, they would merely obstruct his plans to dismantle the city and destroy everything of military value. After all, Sherman did not mean to stay in the city for long, because the Army of Tennessee lurked in Georgia, and Sherman had another plan to further weaken the Army of Northern Virginia and help Grant by laying waste to eastern Georgia and the Carolinas.

Thus, Sherman needed Atlanta's civilians to leave, but he also knew it would be a sensitive topic even among members of the federal government. As such, he wrote about the reasons for doing so back to Halleck in Washington:

"It is sufficient for my Government to know that the removal of the inhabitants has been made with liberality and fairness, that it has been attended with no force, and that no women or children have suffered, unless for want of provisions by their natural protectors and friends.

My real reasons for this step were:

We want all the houses of Atlanta for military storage and occupation.

We want to contract the lines of defense, so as to diminish the garrison to the limit necessary to defend its narrow and vital parts, instead of embracing, as the lines now do, the vast suburbs. This contraction of the lines, with the necessary citadels and redoubts, will make it necessary to destroy the very houses used by families as residences.

Atlanta is a fortified town, was stubbornly defended, and fairly captured. As captors, we have a right to it.

The residence here of a poor population would compel us, sooner or later, to feed them or to see them starve under our eyes.

The residence here of the families of our enemies would be a temptation and a means to keep up a correspondence dangerous and hurtful to our cause; a civil population calls for provost-guards, and absorbs the attention of officers in listening to everlasting complaints and special grievances that are not military.

These are my reasons; and, if satisfactory to the Government of the United States, it makes no difference whether it pleases General Hood and his people or not."

The War Department assented, and Halleck wrote back to him:

"GENERAL: Your communications of the 20th in regard to the removal of families from Atlanta, and the exchange of prisoners, and also the official report of your campaign, are just received. I have not had time as yet to examine your report. The course which you have pursued in removing rebel families from Atlanta, and in the exchange of prisoners, is fully approved by the War Department. Not only are you justified by the laws and usages of war in removing these people, but I think it was your duty to your own army to do so. Moreover, I am fully of opinion that the nature of your position, the character of the war, the conduct of the enemy (and especially of non-combatants and women of the territory which we have heretofore conquered and occupied), will justify you in gathering up all the forage and provisions which your army may require, both for a siege of Atlanta and for your supply in your march farther into the enemy's country. Let the disloyal families of the country, thus stripped, go to their husbands, fathers, and natural protectors, in the rebel ranks; we have tried three years of conciliation and kindness without any reciprocation; on the contrary, those thus treated have acted as spies and guerrillas in our rear and within our lines. The safety of our armies, and a proper regard for the lives of our soldiers, require that we apply to our inexorable foes the severe rules of war."

Naturally, the other side didn't view things the way the federal government and Sherman did, and when Sherman notified Hood of his "evacuation" plans, Hood appealed to God and humanity that Sherman would reconsider: "[S]ir, permit me to say that the unprecedented measure you propose transcends, in studied and ingenious cruelty, all acts ever before brought to my attention in the dark history of war. In the name of God and humanity, I protest, believing that you will find that you are expelling from their homes and firesides the wives and children of a brave people."

Sherman's response to Hood tersely underlined more than his thoughts on war:

"In the name of common-sense, I ask you not to appeal to a just God in such a sacrilegious manner. You who, in the midst of peace and prosperity, have plunged a nation into war—dark and cruel war—who dared and badgered us to battle, insulted our flag, seized our arsenals and forts that were left in the honorable custody of peaceful ordnance-sergeants, seized and made 'prisoners of war' the very garrisons sent to protect your people against negroes and Indians, long before any overt act was committed by the (to you) hated Lincoln Government; tried to force Kentucky and Missouri into rebellion, spite of themselves; falsified the vote of Louisiana; turned loose your privateers to plunder unarmed ships; expelled Union families by the thousands, burned their houses, and declared, by an act of your Congress, the confiscation of all debts due Northern men for goods had and received! Talk thus to the marines, but not to me, who have seen these things, and who will this day make as much sacrifice for the peace and honor of the South as the best-born Southerner among you! If we must be enemies, let us be men, and fight it out as we propose to do, and not deal in arch hypocritical appeals to God and humanity. God will judge us in due time, and he will pronounce whether it be more humane to fight with a town full of women and the families of a brave people at our back or to remove them in time to places of safety among their own friends and people."[13]

Similarly, town leaders in Atlanta begged Sherman to revoke the order expelling Atlanta's citizens:

"We only refer to a few facts, to try to illustrate in part how this measure will operate in practice. As you advanced, the people north of this fell back; and before

---

[13] *Memoirs of General Sherman,* http://www.gutenberg.org/files/4361/4361-h/4361-h.htm

your arrival here, a large portion of the people had retired south, so that the country south of this is already crowded, and without houses enough to accommodate the people, and we are informed that many are now staying in churches and other out-buildings.

This being so, how is it possible for the people still here (mostly women and children) to find any shelter? And how can they live through the winter in the woods—no shelter or subsistence, in the midst of strangers who know them not, and without the power to assist them much, if they were willing to do so?

This is but a feeble picture of the consequences of this measure. You know the woe, the horrors, and the suffering, cannot be described by words; imagination can only conceive of it, and we ask you to take these things into consideration.

We know your mind and time are constantly occupied with the duties of your command, which almost deters us from asking your attention to this matter, but thought it might be that you had not considered this subject in all of its awful consequences, and that on more reflection you, we hope, would not make this people an exception to all mankind, for we know of no such instance ever having occurred—surely never in the United States—and what has this helpless people done, that they should be driven from their homes, to wander strangers and outcasts, and exiles, and to subsist on charity?

We do not know as yet the number of people still here; of those who are here, we are satisfied a respectable number, if allowed to remain at home, could subsist for several months without assistance, and a respectable number for a much longer time, and who might not need assistance at any time.

In conclusion, we most earnestly and solemnly petition you to reconsider this order, or modify it, and suffer this unfortunate people to remain at home, and enjoy what little means they have."

To them, Sherman responded bluntly, and the response included one of his most notorious quotes about war:

"GENTLEMEN: I have your letter of the 11th, in the nature of a petition to revoke my orders removing all the inhabitants from Atlanta. I have read it carefully, and give full credit to your statements of the distress that will be occasioned, and yet shall not revoke my orders, because they were not designed to meet the humanities of the case, but to prepare for the future struggles in which millions of good people outside of Atlanta have a deep interest. We must have peace, not only at Atlanta, but in all America. To secure this, we must stop the war that now desolates our once happy and favored country. To stop war, we must defeat the rebel armies which are arrayed against the laws and Constitution that all must respect and obey. To defeat those armies, we must prepare the way to reach them in their recesses, provided with the arms and instruments which enable us to accomplish our purpose. Now, I know the vindictive nature of our enemy, that we may have many years of military operations from this quarter; and, therefore, deem it wise and prudent to prepare in time. The use of Atlanta for warlike purposes is inconsistent with its character as a home for families. There will be no manufactures, commerce, or agriculture here, for the maintenance of families, and sooner or later want will compel the inhabitants to go. Why not go now, when all the arrangements are completed for the transfer,—instead of waiting till the plunging shot of contending armies will renew the scenes of the past months. Of course, I do not apprehend any such thing at this moment, but you do not suppose this army will be here until the war is over. I cannot discuss this subject with you fairly, because I cannot impart to you what we propose to do, but I assert that our military plans make it necessary for the inhabitants to go away, and I can only renew my offer of services to make their exodus in any direction as easy and comfortable as possible.

You cannot qualify war in harsher terms than I will. War is cruelty, and you cannot refine it; and those who brought war into our country deserve all the curses and maledictions a people can pour out. I know I had no hand in making this war, and I know I will make more sacrifices to-day than any of you to secure peace. But you cannot have peace and a division of our country. If the United States submits to a division now, it will not stop, but will go on until we reap the fate of Mexico, which is eternal war. The United States does and must assert its authority, wherever it once had power; for, if it relaxes one bit to pressure, it is gone, and I believe that such is the national feeling. This feeling assumes various shapes, but always comes back to that of Union. Once admit the Union, once more acknowledge the authority of the national Government, and, instead of devoting your houses and streets and roads to the dread uses of war, I and this army become at once your protectors and supporters, shielding you from danger, let it come from what quarter it may. I know that a few individuals cannot resist a torrent of error and passion, such as swept the South into rebellion, but you can point out, so that we may know those who desire a government, and those who insist on war and its desolation.

You might as well appeal against the thunder-storm as against these terrible hardships of war. They are inevitable, and the only way the people of Atlanta can hope once more to live in peace and quiet at home, is to stop the war, which can only be done by admitting that it began in error and is perpetuated in pride.

We don't want your negroes, or your horses, or your houses, or your lands, or any thing you have, but we do want and will have a just obedience to the laws of the United States. That we will have, and, if it involves the destruction of your improvements, we cannot help it.

You have heretofore read public sentiment in your newspapers, that live by falsehood and excitement; and the quicker you seek for truth in other quarters, the better. I repeat then that, by the original compact of Government, the United States had certain rights in Georgia, which have never been relinquished and never will be; that the South began war by seizing forts, arsenals, mints, custom-houses, etc., etc., long before Mr. Lincoln was installed, and before the South had one jot or tittle of provocation. I myself have seen in Missouri, Kentucky, Tennessee, and Mississippi, hundreds and thousands of women and children fleeing from your armies and desperadoes, hungry and with bleeding feet. In Memphis, Vicksburg, and Mississippi, we fed thousands upon thousands of the families of rebel soldiers left on our hands, and whom we could not see starve. Now that war comes home to you; you feel very different. You deprecate its horrors, but did not feel them when you sent car-loads of soldiers and ammunition, and moulded shells and shot, to carry war into Kentucky and Tennessee, to desolate the homes of hundreds and thousands of good people who only asked to live in peace at their old homes, and under the Government of their inheritance. But these comparisons are idle. I want peace, and believe it can only be reached through union and war, and I will ever conduct war with a view to perfect and early success.

But, my dear sirs, when peace does come, you may call on me for any thing. Then will I share with you the last cracker, and watch with you to shield your homes and families against danger from every quarter.

Now you must go, and take with you the old and feeble, feed and nurse them, and build for them, in more quiet places, proper habitations to shield them against the weather until the mad passions of men cool down, and allow the Union and peace once more to settle over your old homes at Atlanta."

A picture of the last train of civilians leaving Atlanta

A picture of the ruins of Atlanta's First Union Station Depot

In addition to the order expelling Atlanta's citizens, Sherman became despised in the South for the burning of Atlanta, a scene immortalized in Hollywood by movies like *Gone With the Wind*. In reality, the notorious fire that destroyed so much of the city began during the brief siege. In about a month's worth of fighting around the city, the Union armies fired over 100,000 shots at Confederates in the city. At one point during the siege, Sherman reported to Halleck, "The City seems to have a line around it at an average distance to the center of town of about one-and-a-half miles, but our shot passing over this line will destroy the town." On another occasion, he mentioned, "As I write our heavy artillery is at work, and large fires are burning in Atlanta." One

One Union soldier, Charles Fessenden Morse, described the damage done by the shelling in a letter to his brother: "Our shells destroyed a great deal of property. I am sorry now that a single one was thrown into the city. I don't think it hastened the surrender by a day, it did no harm to the rebel army, the only casualties being twenty harmless old men, women, and children, and two soldiers. There are differences of opinion about this kind of warfare, but I don't like it."

Furthermore, though bitter Southerners would later ignore it, the fires and destruction wreaked upon Atlanta was conducted in part by Confederate soldiers who burned and detonated what they could not carry. In his own memoirs, Hood explained that he had to take those kinds of actions to constrain Sherman in the wake of the Confederate defeat and the decision to head north to Tennessee and not defend the rest of Georgia: "I shall make dispositions to prevent the enemy, as far as possible, from foraging south of Atlanta, and at the same time endeavor to prevent his massing supplies at that place. I deem it important that the prisoners at Andersonville should be so disposed of, as not to prevent this Army from moving in any direction it may be thought best. According to all human calculations, we should have saved Atlanta had the officers and men of the Army done what was expected of them. It has been God's will for it to be otherwise. I am of good heart, and feel that we shall yet succeed. The Army is much in need of a little rest. After removing the prisoners from Andersonville, I think we should, as soon as practicable, place our Army upon the communications of the enemy, drawing our supplies from the West Point and Montgomery Railroad."

In fact, on their way out of town, the Confederates torched a train carrying dozens of cars worth of munitions, igniting a giant explosion that destroyed just about everything within a quarter of a mile. As Sherman pointed out in his memoirs, Union soldiers spent their first few weeks in Atlanta making repairs to places and things of military value that the Confederates had destroyed during their retreat: "By the middle of September, matters and things had settled down in Atlanta, so that we felt perfectly at home. The telegraph and railroads were repaired, and we had uninterrupted communication to the rear. The trains arrived with regularity and dispatch, and brought us ample supplies. General Wheeler had been driven out of Middle Tennessee, escaping south across the Tennessee River at Bainbridge; and things looked as though we were to have a period of repose."

Chapter 4: Leaving Atlanta in Ruins

"We cannot change the hearts of those people of the South, but we can make war so terrible that would they will realize the fact that however brave and gallant and devoted to their country, still they are mortal and should exhaust all peaceful remedies before they fly to war."[14] - Sherman

General Hood still commanded an Army of Tennessee that was about half of the strength of Sherman's command, more than 30,000, and he intended to force Sherman away from what Confederate president Jefferson Davis and his military generals thought would be Sherman's next objectives: Augusta or Macon. The Confederates assumed the Union would target those important arsenals or Andersonville, the prison camp that held around 30,000 sickly Union prisoners. Thus, Hood maneuvered to draw Sherman out of Atlanta and hopefully out of Georgia altogether. During October 1864, he looked to have just done just that; for Sherman's army, recently reorganized, gave chase to Hood's northward march, first through Alabama and then into Tennessee. With Hood's use of General Joseph Wheeler's cavalry to cut the railroad tracks that supplied Sherman's armies, it did look like Hood was causing problems for Sherman; and even he had to admit to General Grant that the Confederates ruined 8 miles of track a day, causing a scale of damage to the railroad that would take thousands of workmen to repair.

Sherman's reluctance to chase Hood more avidly worried several Union generals and even the president. General Joseph Hooker, smarting over his perceived slight by the appointment of Oliver Howard over himself, called Sherman "crazy" for not engaging and destroying Hood's Army of Tennessee, and Sherman's steadfast supporting general, Major General George H. Thomas, feared that Sherman had committed a grievous mistake by allowing Hood to get behind his armies and between the supply lines in Chattanooga, Tennessee. President Lincoln feared that one misstep by Sherman -- something Hood was counting on through his escape out of Sherman's clutches in Georgia -- would suffer a calamitous disaster.

In fact, it was probably unfair to doubt Sherman's judgment, and part of the reason he maneuvered so reluctantly was that he knew Hood was erratic. Sherman also knew how much the stakes had been raised since his ability to capture Atlanta, and none more so than for the Lincoln's re-election. Knowing this, and that the autumn rains might arrive and trap his army in the Georgian red clays, Sherman decided to mostly stay in and around Atlanta until the election.

---

[14] Bailey, Ann J. *War and Ruin: William T. Sherman and the Savannah Campaign.* xiv.

Admittedly, this flew in the face of conventional wisdom, which prized attempts to capture key cities and destroy entire armies, but Sherman didn't take Hood's invasion of Tennessee all that seriously and felt Thomas would be able to deal with Hood alone.

Except for Joseph Wheeler's cavalry and Hardee's garrison at Savannah, Georgia had little to stand in the way of Sherman's 60,000 men, and the way Sherman intended to assault Georgia with two simultaneous wings (the left wing towards Augusta, the right in the direction of Macon) meant to violate all the Georgia countryside, not just the cities. Sherman was also targeting too much territory to defend, so Special Field Orders No. 120 reorganized the armies for the purpose of living off the land and supply lines were left behind. For the soldiers to move quickly, they abandoned their heavy supplies of tents and bedrolls, and aside from carrying 40 rounds of ammunition, an undefended Georgia would provide food and other supplies to the fast-moving invaders.

Furthermore, in the special orders, Sherman outlined how he intended to wage war against Georgia.

"I. For the purpose of military operations, this army is divided into two wings viz.: The right wing, Major-General O. O. Howard commanding, composed of the Fifteenth and Seventeenth Corps; the left wing, Major-General H. W. Slocum commanding, composed of the Fourteenth and Twentieth Corps.

II. The habitual order of march will be, wherever practicable, by four roads, as nearly parallel as possible, and converging at points hereafter to be indicated in orders. The cavalry, Brigadier-General Kilpatrick commanding, will receive special orders from the commander-in-chief.

III. There will be no general train of supplies, but each corps will have its ammunition-train and provision-train, distributed habitually as follows: Behind each regiment should follow one wagon and one ambulance; behind each brigade should follow a due proportion of ammunition - wagons, provision-wagons, and ambulances. In case of danger, each corps commander should change this order of march, by having his advance and rear brigades unencumbered by wheels. The separate columns will start habitually at 7 a.m., and make about fifteen miles per day, unless otherwise fixed in orders."[15]

Sherman was certainly inclined to engage in total war, but Grant himself had instructed him similarly: "Take all provisions, forage and stock wanted for the use of your command. Such as cannot be consumed, destroy. Leave the valley so barren that crows flying over it . . . will have

---

[15] William T. Sherman, *Military Division of the Mississippi Special Field Order 120, November 9, 1864*

to carry their provender with them."[16] Sherman certainly took that advice to heart, and the following points in the special field orders would result in vast destruction across Georgia:

"IV. The army will forage liberally on the country during the march. To this end, each brigade commander will organize a good and sufficient foraging party, under the command of one or more discreet officers, who will gather, near the route traveled, corn or forage of any kind, meat of any kind, vegetables, corn-meal, or whatever is needed by the command, aiming at all times to keep in the wagons at least ten day's provisions for the command and three days' forage. Soldiers must not enter the dwellings of the inhabitants, or commit any trespass, but during a halt or a camp they may be permitted to gather turnips, potatoes, and other vegetables, and to drive in stock of their camp. To regular foraging parties must be instructed the gathering of provisions and forage at any distance from the road traveled.

V. To army corps commanders alone is intrusted the power to destroy mills, houses, cotton-gins, &c., and for them this general principle is laid down: In districts and neighborhoods where the army is unmolested no destruction of such property should be permitted; but should guerrillas or bushwhackers molest our march, or should the inhabitants burn bridges, obstruct roads, or otherwise manifest local hostility, then army commanders should order and enforce a devastation more or less relentless according to the measure of such hostility.

VI. As for horses, mules, wagons, &c., belonging to the inhabitants, the cavalry and artillery may appropriate freely and without limit, discriminating, however, between the rich, who are usually hostile, and the poor or industrious, usually neutral or friendly. Foraging parties may also take mules or horses to replace the jaded animals of their trains, or to serve as pack-mules for the regiments or bridges. In all foraging, of whatever kind, the parties engaged will refrain from abusive or threatening language, and may, where the officer in command thinks proper, give written certificates of the facts, but no receipts, and they will endeavor to leave with each family a reasonable portion for their maintenance."[17]

Naturally, a campaign that would be predicated on devastating the countryside would begin with a thorough destruction of everything in Atlanta that Sherman believed could benefit the South militarily. With the campaign slated to start on November 15, Sherman made plans to destroy what he deemed necessary on the 14th, but things did not go according to plan. In his memoirs, he wrote: "Colonel Poe, United States Engineers, of my staff, had been busy in his

---

[16] Gaffney, P. and D. Gaffney. *The Civil War: Exploring History One week at a Time.* Page 360.

[17] William T. Sherman, *Military Division of the Mississippi Special Field Order 120, November 9, 1864*

special task of destruction. He had a large force at work, had leveled the great depot, round house, and the machine-shops of the Georgia Railroad, and had applied fire to the wreck. One of these machine-shops had been used by the rebels as an arsenal, and in it were stored piles of shot and shell, some of which proved to be loaded, and that night was made hideous by the bursting of shells, whose fragments came uncomfortably, near Judge Lyon's house, in which I was quartered. The fire also reached the block of stores near the depot, and the heart of the city was in flames all night, but the fire did not reach the parts of Atlanta where the court-house was, or the great mass of dwelling houses…I remained in Atlanta during the 15th with the Fourteenth Corps, and the rear-guard of the right wing, to complete the loading of the trains, and the destruction of the buildings of Atlanta which could be converted to hostile uses."

Sherman's description may have been short on details, but others were so amazed by the sight that they aptly filled in the blanks. Morse wrote to his brother that the burning of Atlanta was a "magnificent and awful spectacle. For miles around the country was light as day…the flames shooting up for hundreds of feet into the air." As a nearby army band played near him, he told his brother, "It was like fiddling over the burning of Rome."

A contemporary illustration of the burning of Atlanta

Pictures of ruins across Atlanta

Although Sherman indirectly attributed some of the destruction to Confederate munitions, Poe had written back to Washington about receiving Sherman's instructions and that "Atlanta will have ceased to exist" by the time the letter arrived. As Poe's letter suggests, the men under Sherman's command understood that the general would largely accept and overlook the actions taken by individual soldiers, some of whom no doubt had a propensity to get drunk and unruly when not actively campaigning. Sherman had once told a soldier that he was helpless to prevent his men from setting fires: "Can't be stopped…There are men who do this. Set as many guards as you please, they will slip in and set fire."

Other soldiers were more specific about the destruction and admitted to setting fires, in part because they believed they were justified. One Indiana sergeant jotted down in his diary: "The entire city was destroyed [but] for a few occupied houses. It reminds me of the destruction of Babylon … because of the wickedness of her people." One soldier from Michigan confided that he was about to start a fire but stopped himself at the last second: "As I was about to fire one place a little girl about ten years old came to me and said, 'Mr. Soldier you would not burn our house would you? If you did where would we live?' She looked at me with such a pleading look that…I dropped the torch and walked away."

Some Union soldiers admitted to being disgusted by what took place in Atlanta. One Wisconsin soldier wrote, "I believe this destruction of private property in Atlanta was entirely unnecessary and therefore…disgraceful…The cruelties practiced on this campaign towards citizens have been enough to blast a more sacred cause than ours…There certainly is a lack of discipline."

Sherman was characteristically circumspect about the extent of the damage in Atlanta, in keeping with the way he admitted to being unconcerned about the hardships total war brought to the South, but others meticulously tracked the destruction. Only about 10% of Atlanta's private residences were left standing (400 out of 3600), and while Colonel Poe reported that about 40% of the entire city was destroyed, others claimed the destruction was nearly comprehensive. Morse recalled that the only parts of Atlanta left standing were "churches the city hall and the private dwellings. You could hardly find a vestige of the once splendid R.R. depots, warehouses, &c. It was melancholy, but it was war, prosecuted in deadly earnest." One Indiana soldier wrote that Sherman's men "utterly destroyed Atlanta," and Hood would point out in his memoirs that Sherman informed Grant he had "made a wreck of Atlanta." Sherman even made reference to "deliberately destroy[ing] Atlanta" in an order read to his men after the successful conclusion of the March to the Sea.

Morse would tell his brother that the fire had left Atlanta "of no more importance than the most insignificant town in Georgia," and of course, that was Sherman's objective all along. Sherman would write nostalgically about leaving Atlanta at the start of the campaign, but not out of any sense of regard for the city itself: "Atlanta was soon lost behind the screen of trees, and became a thing of the past. Around it clings many a thought of desperate battle, of hope and fear, that now seem like the memory of a dream; and I have never seen the place since. The day was extremely beautiful, clear sunlight, with bracing air, and an unusual feeling of exhilaration seemed to pervade all minds--a feeling of something to come, vague and undefined, still full of venture and intense interest. Even the common soldiers caught the inspiration, and many a group called out to me as I worked my way past them, 'Uncle Billy, I guess Grant is waiting for us at Richmond!'"

In the over 150 years since the burning of Atlanta, the recriminations have been pointed in just about every conceivable direction. To a degree, everyone is wrong and everyone is right, because there was no real way to document which damage was done by the Confederates and which was done by Sherman. As Sherman biographer John F. Marszalek points out, "But the historical facts are clear that the entire city was not destroyed and Sherman was not solely responsible for the part that was. Hood had destroyed numerous houses during his defense of the city and his evacuation in September…Hood's army exploded 80 cars of filled with ammunition, and as a later historian has phrased it, 'the smoke and resulting fires [were] partially responsible for the loss of many homes and buildings later said to have been burned by Sherman.'"

An 1865 picture of some of the ruins in Atlanta

It would be impossible to determine just how much damage Sherman wrought on Atlanta and during his infamous March to the Sea. Sherman put the total amount of destruction around $100 million worth, the equivalent of about $1.5 billion today, and his men wrecked hundreds of miles of railroad and telegraph lines while taking thousands of mules, horses and cattle. Sherman's men also seized millions of pounds of corn and other foodstuffs, all while destroying a countless amount of private citizens' properties and industries.

Sherman was also acutely aware of the psychological success of his campaigns in Georgia. In a letter to Halleck on Christmas Eve 1864, Sherman summed up the rationale that has compelled many to consider him the first modern general and a harbinger of total warfare: "We are not only fighting armies, but a hostile people, and must make old and young, rich and poor, feel the hard hand of war, as well as their organized armies. I know that this recent movement of mine through Georgia has had a wonderful effect in this respect. Thousands who had been deceived by their lying papers into the belief that we were being whipped all the time, realized the truth, and have no appetite for a repetition of the same experience."

In that regard, he was certainly right. After the destruction of Atlanta, a similar fate would be visited upon Columbia, South Carolina in early 1865, and the war would be over shortly thereafter.

Online Resources

Other books about the Civil War by Charles River Editors

Other books about the Atlanta Campaign

Bibliography

Bailey, Anne J. The Chessboard of War: Sherman and Hood in the Atlanta Campaign of 1864. Lincoln, NE: University of Nebraska Press, 2000. ISBN 978-0-8032-1273-2.

Bonds, Russell S. War Like the Thunderbolt: The Battle and Burning of Atlanta. Yardley, PA: Westholme Publishing, 2009. ISBN 978-1-59416-100-1.

Campbell, Jacqueline Glass. When Sherman Marched North from the Sea: Resistance on the Confederate Home Front. Chapel Hill: University of North Carolina Press, 2003. ISBN 978-0-8078-5659-8.

Castel, Albert. Decision in the West: The Atlanta Campaign of 1864. Lawrence: University Press of Kansas, 1992. ISBN 0-7006-0748-X.

Catton, Bruce. The Centennial History of the Civil War. Vol. 3, Never Call Retreat. Garden City, NY: Doubleday, 1965. ISBN 0-671-46990-8.

Davis, Stephen, What the Yankees Did to Us: Sherman's Bombardment and Wrecking of Atlanta. Macon, GA: Mercer University Press, 2012.

Eicher, David J. The Longest Night: A Military History of the Civil War. New York: Simon & Schuster, 2001. ISBN 0-684-84944-5.

Glatthaar, Joseph T. The March to the Sea and Beyond: Sherman's Troops in the Savannah and Carolinas Campaigns. New York: New York University Press, 1985. ISBN 0-8147-3001-9.

Hattaway, Herman, and Archer Jones. How the North Won: A Military History of the Civil War. Urbana: University of Illinois Press, 1983. ISBN 0-252-00918-5.

Hess, Earl J. Kennesaw Mountain: Sherman, Johnston and the Atlanta Campaign. Chapel Hill: University of North Carolina Press, 2013. ISBN 978-1-4696-0211-0.

Kennett, Lee. Marching through Georgia: The Story of Soldiers and Civilians During

Sherman's Campaign. New York: HarperCollins Publishers, 1995. ISBN 0-06-092745-3.

McPherson, James M. Battle Cry of Freedom: The Civil War Era. Oxford History of the United States. New York: Oxford University Press, 1988. ISBN 0-19-503863-0.

Miles, Jim. To the Sea: A History and Tour Guide of the War in the West, Sherman's March across Georgia and through the Carolinas, 1864–1865. Nashville, TN: Cumberland House, 2002. ISBN 1-58182-261-8.

Nevin, David, and the Editors of Time-Life Books. Sherman's March: Atlanta to the Sea. Alexandria, VA: Time-Life Books, 1986. ISBN 0-8094-4812-2.

Rose, Willie Lee. Rehearsal for Reconstruction: The Port Royal Experiment. Indianapolis: Bobbs-Merrill, 1964.

Sherman, William T. Memoirs of General W.T. Sherman. 2nd ed. New York: Library of America, 1990. ISBN 0-940450-65-8. First published 1889 by D. Appleton & Co.

Trudeau, Noah Andre. Southern Storm: Sherman's March to the Sea. New York: HarperCollins, 2008. ISBN 978-0-06-059867-9.

U.S. War Department, The War of the Rebellion: a Compilation of the Official Records of the Union and Confederate Armies. Washington, DC: U.S. Government Printing Office, 1880–1901.

Woodworth, Steven E. *Jefferson Davis and His Generals: The Failure of Confederate Command in the West.* Lawrence: University Press of Kansas, 1990.